The 7 Topics
Therapy Workbook
by
Ophelia Ramirez-Mailloux,
MSW, LISW-S

Copyright 2013

The 7 Topics Therapy Workbook
by
Ophelia Ramirez-Mailloux,
MSW, LISW-S

I am a Licensed Independent Social Worker (LISW-S). And I currently work as a Mental Health/Behavioral Health Therapist. I created this workbook to use with my own clientele. And I thought it would be a nice gesture to share this information with other therapists as well, so they do not have to reinvent the *wheel*, so to speak. Pun intended. You will understand what I mean as you keep reading…

I understand that not every client is going to have the same problems. However, over time, I noticed that there was a pattern, that many of the clients shared the same problems or life stressors.

Also I believe that there are primarily 7 Topics that most situations fall under:
1) Individual - a) Body b) Mind c) Soul
2) House/Housing
3) Car/Transportation
4) Job/Career/College
5) Money/Finances
6) Relationships
7) Fun

And I believe that if people will take a look at those 7 areas; see where the problems are; and then trouble shoot in those areas, that their lives would run smoother. And it would help them to be goal-oriented, more well-rounded as individuals, and thus, happier individuals.

So you will see that, throughout this workbook, the 7 Topics are at the heart of the interventions.

And also, just as teachers come up with a curriculum for their students, I believe that we too can come up with such a plan as well. However, based on the client's answers to the very first workbook page, you will discover that the plan will become tailored to meet their individual needs.

I hope you find this workbook as helpful as I have found it to be for me and my clients.

And by all means, please, feel free to copy the **worksheets** for your sessions to be used with your clients. That is what I created this for and that is what you paid for. However, please, respect the book in its entirety. In other words, let other therapists buy their own copies of the actual workbook and thus, the worksheets as well. I made sure to make this affordable for this very reason. I had this copy written and I hope you will respect that.

Also, just a note, THIS BOOK IS NOT JUST FOR THERAPISTS TO USE WITH THEIR CLIENTS. ANYBODY COULD BENEFIT FROM USING THIS BOOK FOR THEMSELVES, AS A SELF HELP BOOK.

Thank you and enjoy.

Ophelia Ramirez-Mailloux, LISW-S

What You Will Find on the Following Pages:

- How to use the 7 Topics Wheel of Life Stressors, along with the Questions pages that leads you around the wheel.

- How to use the Problem Solving Sheets

Then after that comes the Worksheets:

1. The 7 Topics Wheel of Life Stressors (1pg)
2. The 7 Topics Blank "Why" Wheel (1pg)
3. The 7 Topics List of Possible Life Stressors for Adults (3 pgs)
4. The 7 Topics List of Possible Life Stressors for Teens/Children (3pgs)
5. The 7 Topics List of Problem Solving/Solutions pages for Adults or Teens/Children (2 pgs)
6. An Example of a completed Wheel of Life Stressors (1pg)
7. The Example completed Problem Solving pages to go with the example Wheel of Life Stressors (2pgs).
8. The 7 Topics Goals pages with example goals (10 pgs)

How to use The 7 Topics Wheel of Life Stressors

You print off a copy of the **The 7 Topics Wheel of Life Stressors** and lay it on your desk for you and your client to see.

Then use **The 7 Topics List of Possible Life Stressors Question** Pages. **There is one for Adults and one for Teens/Children. You ask the questions,** while the client answers. Some of the questions you will already know the answer to because, at this point, you have completed an assessment with them and gathered their history.

You will be transferring their answers onto **The 7 Topics Wheel of Life Stressors/ Why am I coming to therapy page.**

How to use the Problem Solving Pages
Once the Wheel is complete, beginning at topic #1 on the Wheel of Life Stressors, you go around the wheel and you both brain storm together to come up with possible solutions.

You record the possible solutions onto **The 7 Topics Problem Solving** pages, which is also separated into the 7 topics. This process helps them be involved and to see where the issues are in every area of their lives, and they are involved in the problem solving process as well.

The things that you list for possible solutions should keep you busy for quite a few sessions. You go down the list, session after session, reviewing whatever solution you came up with, which might include, a handout; a short video clip or whatever you have planned as a possible solution to help them with that life stressor.

And remember some of the identified life stressors might need a Why Wheel of its own, and that could take you off into more possible solutions.

So to recap:

- You both look through the 7 Topics Life Stressors pages together

- Then you record on the 7 Topics Wheel of Life Stressors/Why am I Coming to Therapy Wheel. You both identify what their current main life stressors are and thus, why they are in therapy.

- You come up with possible solutions, together, but as a therapist you might have handouts and ideas that the client might not know about. That's why they have sought out the help of a therapist.

- Each session, you just keep reviewing things that can help them ie, under the "mind" topic. If they listed depression, anxiety, trauma, self-esteem, grief, alcohol addiction, etc, just think of all the handouts or resources that you could review with them as they come to therapy sessions.

- Also, a special note, many times, once you have completed the wheel with clients, you will discover that the client has need of some type of resource ie, help with clothing, rent, transportation, referral to Welfare or Department of Jobs and Family Services for medical insurance, such as, the medical card; need for food, such as, food stamps; need for employment, such as help with a resume, job searches, etc.

- I keep a Resource Check List that I complete with clients about what resources they might need. Then I provide them with a handout that lists many of our local agencies that can provide those needed resources.

In the end, this is about getting every area of their lives running as smoothly as possible. You will be helping them to deal with *current* life stressors and/or *past* traumas, and helping them set goals for their *futures.*

Extra

By now, I am sure you have noticed that there are 2 Different Wheels. The first one already has something written in the middle - "Current Life Stressors/Why Am I Coming to Therapy". Because that is the first question that needs answered in order to begin the whole process.

However, please notice the blank "Why" Wheel. It can be used for anything you are trying to understand.

I have found this tool to be priceless. And as you know, not every problem is so easily figured out and easily solved, or people would not need a therapist.
So sometimes a life stressor that a client might identify on the Life Stressors Wheel, might need a "Why" Wheel of its own. For example, if someone listed that one of the reasons they are here for therapy is because they are depressed because Children Services removed their children from their home.
You can help them complete a "Why" Wheel on that stressor which could really help them realize what they did wrong; own up to the responsibility; and to take the steps to fix the problem, in order to get their children back and keep them.

Extra

You will notice that the last handouts have 10 pages. They are called the 7 Topics Goals sheets. I actually created this for myself, for my own life and goals. Then I decided to share it with my clients.

I also encourage them to make a **7 Topics Goal Board** from the topics. For example, I bought a cork board and put the 7 topics headings on the board, leaving enough room to place pictures and quotes under each heading. Then I found pictures, words, etc to represent my goals that I had written for my 7 Topics Goals.

The first one I ever made was back in 1997 when I began college. I bought myself a cheap white poster board, and 2 graduation cards because I knew I wanted my Bachelor's and then my Master's in Social Work.

A little hint: Pictures and words that are used for scrapbooking are perfect for this project.

I keep my 7 Topics Goal Board in my bedroom right by the bed so it is the first thing I see when I get up in the morning and the last thing I see when I go to bed at night. I also pray over it and meditate upon it. I look at the pictures and pray and ask God to lead and guide me regarding making my goals come true.

The Next Page begins the Handouts……

The 7 Topics Wheel of Life Stressors
   1. **Individual**

Body   **Mind**   **Soul**

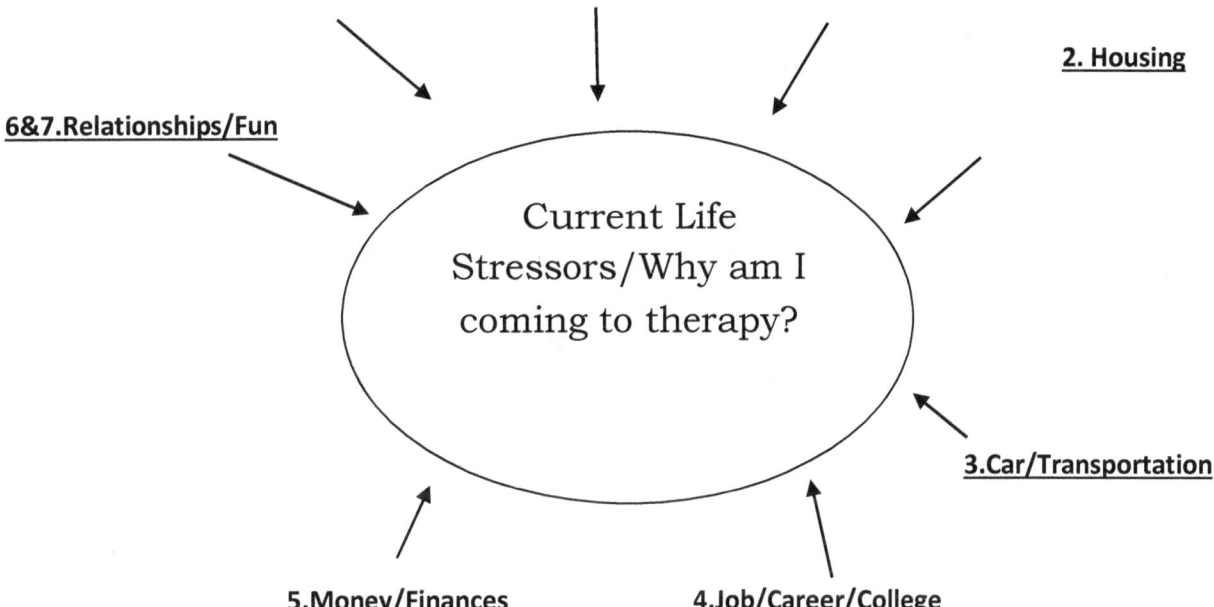

2. Housing

6&7.Relationships/Fun

Current Life
Stressors/Why am I
coming to therapy?

3.Car/Transportation

5.Money/Finances   **4.Job/Career/College**

The 7 Topics Blank "Why" Wheel

1. **Individual**

Body   **Mind**   **Soul**

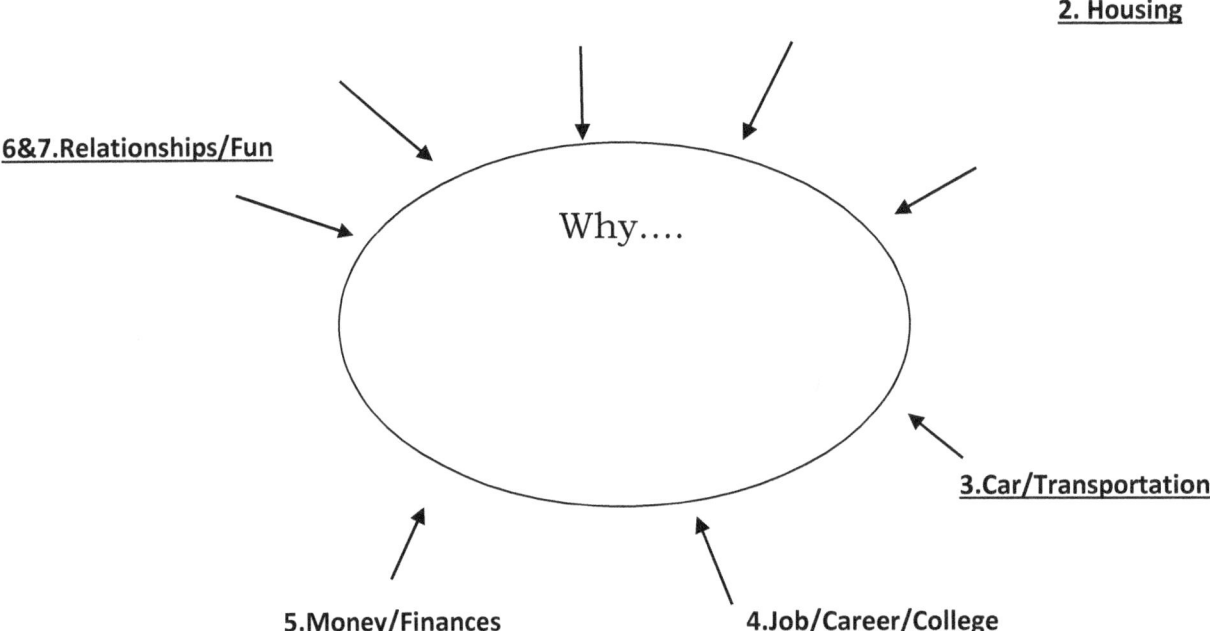

2. Housing

6&7.Relationships/Fun

Why....

3.Car/Transportation

5.Money/Finances   **4.Job/Career/College**

The 7 Topics List of Possible Life Stressors for Adults – Questions Page

A lot of times, Depression and Anxiety are the primary reasons that people seek to go to therapy. And Depression and Anxiety are usually due to LIFE STRESSORS.

 Because everybody's life is not the same, Life Stressors can come in many different forms. However, there are certain stressors that seem to show up time and again in client's lives.

Below is a list of some of those main reasons that clients have come to therapy for.
You will review these with client together, and you will transfer their answers on to the 7 Topics Wheel of Life Stressors. Of course your space will be limited on the wheel, so you will shorten and abbreviate the answers.

BODY
-You have a Specific Physical Health Problem that you are worried about ie, cancer, etc
-You are in Chronic Pain ie back pain due to a car accident or injury, etc.
-You have something wrong with you and they - the Dr's - have not been able to figure out just what it is.
-You have gained weight and cannot seem to lose.
-You are waiting on Social Security Disability Claim
- You have an eating disorder – Anorexia; Bulimia; Stress Eating
- You have major sleep problems that is affecting your ability to function
- You keep having miscarriages or you have been told by a dr that you will never be able to have children
-Other: _____

MIND
-Your main concern is Depression, scale of 1-10, 10 being the worst, you are a: ___
-Your main concern is Anxiety, scale of 1-10, 10 being the worst, you are a: ___
-Maybe you question if you have Bipolar.
-You became involved in Drugs and/or Alcohol or are in remission
-You are in some legal trouble; have court coming up soon; on probation for something and struggle to meet all the demands that are placed on you
-Children Services is involved in your life and you struggle to meet all the demands that are placed on you
-Your Children were taken by Children Services
-Bereavement - someone you love has died in the past year; also someone died due to suicide; someone died due to a traumatic accident; or you had a major breakup
-Self esteem - you have self-esteem issues; or self-loathing.
- Trauma - Abuse - physical; sexual; emotional; Domestic Violence, etc; traumatizing event like a major car accident; held up at gun point, anything where you felt like your life was threatened

- You have Anger Management issues
- You have been diagnosed with or suspect that you have ADHD
-Other: _____

SOUL- I ask them if they have "a goal for their soul"
-You are questioning things that pertain to life and death.
-You are confused about what you believe in
-You can't seem to find any peace and you wonder where God is
-Other: _____

HOUSE/HOUSING
-You are homeless, living from place to place (this falls under financial problems too)
-You are behind in rent and face eviction (this falls under financial problems too)
-Your house is in need of some major repairs and you do not really have the money to fix them (this falls under financial problems too)
-Your landlord is not fixing things as they should.
-Other: _____

CAR/TRANSPORTATION
-You do not have a car so have to use bus, taxi, walk, friends and family drive you (this falls under financial problems too)
-Your car is in need of major repairs and you do not really have the money to fix them (this falls under financial problems too)
-You are behind in car payments and they could repossess your car any day. (this falls under financial problems too)
-You lost your license and you are still driving when you should not, and risk being put in jail if caught.
-Other: _____

JOB/CAREER/COLLEGE
-You lost your job and have not been able to find a new one
-You hate your current job
-You like your job, but you are having trouble with someone at work
-You feel that you cannot work anymore and are thinking of going on Social Security Disability
-You feel that you cannot work anymore, so you have applied to Social Security Disability already and are waiting.
- You are no longer working, but you miss going to work; miss the closeness you had with others at work, miss the feeling of gratification; the rewards of work, etc.
-You can't seem to hold down a job. You either end up getting fired, or you quit.
-You just got out of jail or prison and cannot seem to find a job.
-Other: _____

MONEY/FINANCIAL
-You do not make enough money, to make ends meet.
-You owe child support and you struggle to make it.
-Your wages are being garnished, and you struggle to make it.
-You just got out of jail or prison and cannot seem to find a job, housing, etc.
-The minute you have money, someone wants to "borrow" some from you.
-Other: _____

RELATIONSHIPS
-You feel like someone in your life is making you completely miserable right now.
-You are not sure if you want to stay with your spouse/partner.
- You do not have a partner or spouse and would like to meet someone.
- You are questioning your sexuality (heterosexual, homosexual, bisexual) and are confused, scared to tell others, are married with children and not sure you want to be anymore due to your sexuality, etc. Or others issues surrounding your sexuality.
-Your partner has cheated and you do not know what to do.
-Your partner was involved with someone over the internet or texting, and they do not see it as cheating, but you do because of the things that were said, pictures that were sent, etc.
-Your children are causing you a lot of grief right now ie, they are not going to school, getting into trouble at school; not listening at home; in trouble w/ the law etc.
-You have a strained relationship with your mom, dad, brother, sister, grandparents etc
-You are having an argument with your best friend
-You are having trouble with someone at work/school/college
-Trouble with a neighbor
-Other: _____

FUN
-You do not know what fun is anymore. You have not done anything fun in a very long time.
-You do not have money to go out and do what you consider to be fun.
-Other: _____

The 7 Topics List of Possible Life Stressors for Teens and Children – Questions Page

A lot of times, Depression and Anxiety are the primary reasons that people seek to go to therapy. And Depression and Anxiety are usually due to LIFE STRESSORS.

Because everybody's life is not the same, Life Stressors can come in many different forms. However, there are certain stressors that seem to show up time and again in teenager's/children's lives.
Below is a list of some of those main reasons that Teen/Children clients have come to therapy for.
You will review these with client and guardian together, and you will transfer their answers on to the 7 Topics Why Wheel. Of course your space will be limited on the wheel, so you will shorten and abbreviate the answers.

BODY
-You have a Specific Physical Health Problem that you are worried about
-You are in Chronic Pain
-You have something wrong with you and they - the Dr's - have not been able to figure out just what it is.
-You have gained weight and cannot seem to lose.
-Parents: You are waiting on Social Security Disability Claim for your child/teen
- You have an eating disorder – Anorexia; Bulimia; Stress Eating
- You have major sleep problems that is affecting your ability to function
- You are pregnant and not sure what to do.
- You have low self esteem/body image problems
-Other: _____

MIND
-Your main concern is Depression, scale of 1-10, 10 being the worst, you are a: ___
- You have been cutting as a means of coping with depression or disappointments
-Your main concern is Anxiety, scale of 1-10, 10 being the worst, you are a: ___
-Maybe you question if you have Bipolar or Mood D/O.
-You became involved in Drugs and/or Alcohol – using or selling or both
-You are in some legal trouble; have court coming up soon; on probation for something and struggle to do all the demands that are put on you
-Children Services is involved in your family and you are scared about what is going to happen.
-You are a teen mom, and your Children were taken by Children Services
-Bereavement - someone you love has died in the past year; also someone died due to suicide; someone died due to a traumatic accident; or you had a major breakup
-Self esteem - you have self esteem issues; or self loathing.
- Trauma - Abuse - physical; sexual; emotional; Domestic Violence, etc; traumatizing event like a major car accident; held up at gun point, anything where you felt like your life was threatened

- You have Anger Management issues
- You have been diagnosed with or suspect that you have ADHD
- You have ODD and relational problems with your parents, teachers, adults, etc
-Other: _____

SOUL
-You are questioning things that pertain to life and death.
-You are confused about what you believe
-You can't seem to find any peace and you wonder where God is
-Other: _____

HOUSE/HOUSING/AT HOME
-You are homeless, living from place to place (this falls under financial problems too)
-You know that your family is behind in rent and face eviction and you are scared. (this falls under financial problems too)
- You have ran away from home multiple times. Why? Complete separate why wheel
-Other: _____

CAR/TRANSPORTATION
If you are 16 and old enough to be working and driving. Or you know some of these to be true about your parents/caregivers:
-You do not have a car so have to use bus, taxi, walk, friends and family drive you (this falls under financial problems too)
-Your car is in need of major repairs and you do not really have the money to fix it (this falls under financial problems too)
-You are behind in car payments and they could repossess your car any day. (this falls under financial problems too)
-You lost your license and you are still driving when you should not, and risk being put in jail if caught.
-Other: _____

JOB/SCHOOL
The Job questions pertain to you if you are 16 and old enough to be working
Or you know some of these to be true about your parents/caregivers:
-You lost your job and have not been able to find a new one
-You hate your current job
-You like your job, but you are having trouble with someone at work
- You are no longer working, but you miss going to work; miss the closeness you had with others at work, etc.
-You can't seem to hold down a job. You either end up getting fired, or you quit.
-Other: _____

School

-You have trouble getting up in the mornings to go to school

- You are constantly trying to get out of school by saying you are sick, etc

- You hate school! Why? - Complete separate Why Wheel

- You are being bullied by someone at school

- You are having trouble with a friend, peer, teacher, principal, or other at school.

- Your grades are poor and you struggle in school

-Other: _____

MONEY/FINANCIAL

Some of these questions pertain to you if you are 16 and old enough to be working or you know that these apply to your parents/caregivers.

-You do not make enough money to make ends meet.

-You owe child support and you struggle to make it.

-Your wages are being garnished, and you struggle to make it.

-The minute you have money, someone wants to "borrow" some from you.

-Other: _____

RELATIONSHIPS

-You feel like someone in your life is making you completely miserable right now.

-You are not sure if you want to stay with your partner.

- You do not have a partner and you would like to.

- You are questioning your sexuality (heterosexual, homosexual, bisexual) and are confused, scared to tell others. Or others issues surrounding your sexuality.

-Your partner has cheated and you do not know what to do.

-Your partner was involved with someone over the internet or texting, and they do not see it as cheating, but you do because of the things that were said, pictures that were sent, etc.

-You have a strained relationship with your mom, dad, brother, sister, grandparents etc

-You are having an argument with your best friend or a peer at school

-You are having trouble with someone at work/school

- You are having trouble with bullying at school, online, etc.

-You are having trouble with a neighbor

- You are on probation and struggling

- Children Services is involved in the family and you are worried.

-Other: _____

FUN

-You do not know what fun is anymore. You have not done anything fun in a very long time.

-You or your parents/caregivers do not have money to go out and do what you consider to be fun.

- What you consider fun, your parents/caregivers do not and so you cannot do those things.

-Other: _____

THE 7 TOPICS PROBLEM SOLVING PAGES
(for Adults or Teens/Children)

Body

-

-

-

-

-

Mind

-

-

-

-

-

Soul

-

-

-

-

-

House/Housing

-

-

-

-

-

Car/Transportation

-

-

-

-

-

Job/Career/College

-

-

-

-

-

Money/Finances

-

-

-

-

-

Relationships & Fun

-

-

-

-

-

Example of completed Wheel of Life Stressors

1. Individual

Body   **Mind**   **Soul**

- Diabetes   - Depression   - Grief (mom died)   - I want to explore religion
- HTN   - Anxiety   - Alcohol/DUI   - What am I supposed to do
- Back pain/chronic pain - Trauma/sexual abuse   with my life
- Weight gain/can't seem to lose - Self esteem issues
- Sleep problems

2. Housing

6&7.Relationships/Fun

- strained
relationship w/ spouse

- No fun in life

Current Life Stressors/Why am I coming to therapy?

- need new roof
landlord not fixing

3.Car/Transportation

- lost my license- DUI

5.Money/Finances

- struggle to make it financially

4.Job/Career/College

- lost job due to DUI
- thinking of college

EXAMPLE PROBLEM SOLVING PAGE TO GO WITH EXAMPLE WHEEL OF LIFE STRESSORS

Body

- re: Diabetes, to go to my Dr. on a regular basis; take my meds as Dr. Rx'd.
- My diet can make a difference, so I need to learn how to eat healthy and then do it. Maybe a consult with a Registered Dietician about a diet.
- re: HTN, to go to my Dr. on a regular basis; take my meds as Dr. Rx'd. Also, note that my diet can make a difference with this too, as well as exercise.
- re: back pain/chronic pain - to go to my Dr. on a regular basis; take my meds as Dr. Rx'd or my Dr. could refer me to a pain specialist. Maybe try chiropractic care; Yoga etc.
-re: weight gain and can't seem to lose. The Dr. could test my thyroid or hormones to see if there is something wrong that is keeping me from being able to lose, and gaining too easily.
- I could get a gym membership.
- re: sleep problems, I could talk to my Dr. about my sleep issues to see if they might Rx me something, or try something natural like Melatonin to help me sleep
-

Mind

- re: Depression, anxiety, grief, alcohol abuse, trauma from sexual abuse as a child, and self-esteem issues, I could go see a therapist
- I could read self-help books, like Joel Osteen; Tony Robins
- I could consider talking to my Dr. about an antidepressant or antianxiety med.
- I could go to AA meetings
-

Soul

- re: exploring religions – I could start researching on-line
- I could attend some church services, locally, to see what I think
- I could research colleges and see what they have to offer.
- I could take a test that is supposed to tell you what career you are best suited for based on your personality and likes.

House/Housing

- re: the roof, we need to talk to the landlord again and let them know how bad it is and insist that they come out and take a look at it.
-

Car/Transportation

- re: losing my license to DUI – I can keep paying on my fines so that they are all paid up by the time that the 1 year is up when I can get my license back again.
- I have to learn to use bus transportation and have a few friends/family as back-ups.
- I have the medical card, so there are certain places in town, like Apple Lane, who give

people rides to Dr. appointments.
-

Job/Career/College

- re: losing my job to DUI – I need to update my resume.
- I need to go on several job search web sites ie, Career Builder; Monster, etc. and get signed up for job alerts.
- I could go to the One Stop program through the Department of Job and Family Services and see if they could help me with my resume and job search.
- Again, I could research colleges and what they offer to see if I want to go to college
-

Money/Finances

- re: struggling to make it financially, I could do the job search
- I could research on-line about ways to make extra money ie, sell things on eBay; have a garage sale, etc.
- I could go to Jobs and Family services to see what help I am eligible for ie food stamps, the medical card, etc.
-

Relationships & Fun

- re: strained relationship w/ husband, I could ask him to watch the movie *Fire Proof* with me, and the book that goes with it, called *Love Dare*.
- We could go to therapy together.
- We could read the book *Men are from Mars, Women are from Venus.*
- re: no fun in life, we could start having a date night at least every two weeks when we get paid.
- We could look up things to do in our town, for example in Mansfield Ohio. Look up mansfieldcalendarofevents.com

The 7 Topics Goals List (to use with the 7 Topics Goal Board)

1 - Individual
a) Body
b) Mind
c) Soul

2- House/Housing

3- Car/Transportation

4- Job/Career/College

5- Money/Finances

6- Relationships

7- Fun

To keep your life organized, on task, and goal oriented, use this list to evaluate where you are in your life right now in those areas, and make goals under each topic, accordingly.

Re-evaluate on a regular basis. Your life will feel more organized. You can look back and see the goals you have achieved and then set new ones.

1 - Individual

a) Body

Example of goals: to lose 50 lbs.
Ex: to eat healthier, like the Mediterranean Diet
Ex: to exercise at least 4 times a week, for 30 minutes

b) Mind

Ex: to obtain my GED and/or to go to college
Ex: to go to therapy to work on some of my issues
Ex: to learn how to speak Spanish
Ex: to learn how to play the guitar

c) Soul

Ex: To pray and meditate daily
Ex: to read my Bible daily
Ex: to go to church weekly
Ex: to pay my tithes
Ex: to do a work in the church with the talent that God has given
me

2- House/Housing

Ex: to own my own Tiny House – research Tiny House Movement

3- Car/Transportation

Ex: to own my car – no payments

4- Job/Career/College

Ex: to work at a job in my career, and to enjoy it
Ex: to own my own business

5- Money/Finances

Ex: to pay off all my debt
Ex: to attend a Financial Peace University program by Dave Ramsey in order to find out how to pay off all my debt and prepare for my future

6- Relationships

Ex: to make amends with my sister
Ex: to get married to the right person someday
Ex: to have a few good friends in my life to share life with
Ex: to get involved at church and grow my circle of friends

7- Fun

Ex: to have date night once a month with my spouse/partner
Ex: to have family night once a week with my family
Ex: to have Girl's/Boy's night out once a month with my friends
Ex: to join a volleyball team

Final words:

I hope that you find this workbook useful.

As I said before, most of the worksheets were created for myself, to help create goals and problem solve in my own personal life.

Then I decided "hey, if this works for me, why not use it with my clients".

Then later I said "hey, if this works for me and my clients, why not make a workbook so it can work for others as well".

So here it is ~ happy problem solving and goal setting!

May all your goals come true!

Sincerely,

Ophelia Ramirez-Mailloux, LISW-S